Let's Learn About Adoption

The Adoption Club Therapeutic Workbook on Adoption and Its Many Different Forms

Regina M. Kupecky

Illustrated by Apsley

Jessica Kingsley *Publishers*
London and Philadelphia

First published in 2015
by Jessica Kingsley Publishers
73 Collier Street
London N1 9BE, UK
and
400 Market Street, Suite 400
Philadelphia, PA 19106, USA

www.jkp.com

Library of Congress Cataloging in Publication Data
A CIP catalog record for this book is available from the Library of Congress

British Library Cataloguing in Publication Data
A CIP catalogue record for this book is available from the British Library

ISBN 978 1 84905 762 2
eISBN 978 0 85700 997 5

Printed and bound in Great Britain by Bell & Bain Ltd, Glasgow

MIX
Paper from
responsible sources
FSC
www.fsc.org
FSC® C007785

INTRODUCTION FOR ADULTS

About this series

This workbook is Book 1 of a series of workbooks about The Adoption Club written for social workers, counselors or therapists working with children aged 5–11, as well as adoptive parents.

The five interactive therapeutic workbooks have been written to address the key emotional and psychological challenges they are likely to experience. They provide an approachable, interactive and playful way to help children to learn about themselves and have fun at the same time.

About this book

Let's Learn About Adoption is the first book in the Adoption Club series and introduces different kinds of adoption as well as begins a discussion about feelings and birth parents.

Many families start their adoption story with the day the child arrives. But, before there can be an adoption, there have to be birth parents who were, no matter for how short a time, involved with the child.

Whether you are a parent, a counselor, a therapist, a social worker or a doctor this book will help children by opening the adoption world to them. They will no longer feel alone, because they can find a character whose story resembles theirs.

The story brings up many topics, and completing the workbook will probably take many sessions. The coloring and workbook format helps children express their own feelings in a non-threatening way.

Hopefully the workbook will help the child be able to discuss their own story and their feelings about it.

If you have questions or need help please drop me an email at ReginaKu@msn.com.

Other workbooks in the Adoption Club series

Book 2: *How Do We Feel About Adoption? The Adoption Club Therapeutic Workbook on Feelings and Behavior*

Book 3: *The Confusing World of Brothers, Sisters and Adoption: The Adoption Club Therapeutic Workbook on Siblings*

Book 4: *Friends, Bullies and Staying Safe: The Adoption Club Therapeutic Workbook on Friendship*

Book 5: *Who We Are and Why We Are Special: The Adoption Club Therapeutic Workbook on Identity*

Meet The Adoption Club!

The Adoption Club is made up of many characters whose lives have been touched by adoption.

Mrs. Bright is the counselor who runs the group.

Mr. Jackman is a history teacher who helps. He was adopted as an infant in a closed adoption. That meant growing up he knew nothing about his birth parents. As an adult he searched for them and found them.

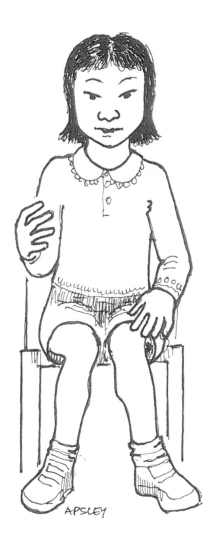

Mary was adopted from China by her single mom. Everyone knows she is adopted because her mom is White and she is Asian. She was three years old when she came to her mom. She is ten right now. She was left by her birth family near the post office in China and then went to an orphanage.

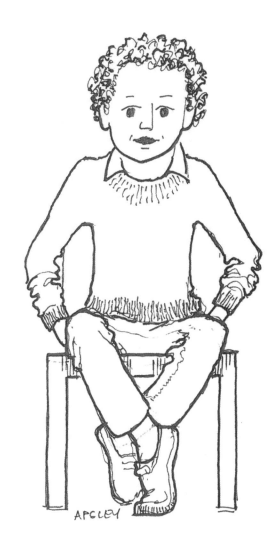

Alexander was adopted from Russia by a single dad. He was five when he joined his family. He lived in an orphanage too.

Alice was adopted in an open adoption as an infant. Her birth mother is of Mexican heritage and her birth father is of Puerto Rican heritage. Her birth parents chose her adoptive parents. She still visits her birth parents. She is nine and has one brother who was born to her adoptive parents.

Angela is nine and her birth brother Michael is thirteen. They lived with their birth parents for many years until they went into foster care. Both lived in several homes, and not always together. They have been in their adoptive family for one year. The family adopted two other children before them, who are now four and six.

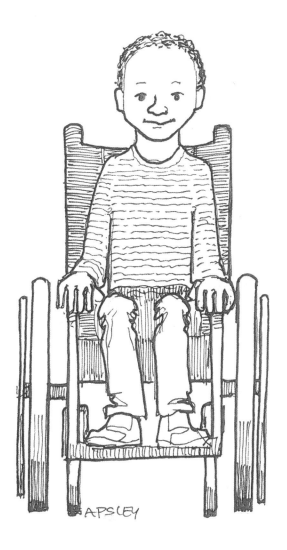

Robert has a disability and needs a wheelchair to get around. He is twelve and was adopted into a kinship adoption, which means he is related to his adoptive family. His adoptive mom is his birth father's sister. They have four birth children and may adopt again. It is a big family.

Let's Learn About Adoption

It was a perfect autumn day when the families began to gather in the school meeting room. The Adoption Club was being called to order.

The children looked around the room. They had no idea so many children from their school were adopted. It felt good to be with people who had adoption in common.

Do you know any other adopted children?

_____

_____

_____

_____

How was their adoption the same or different than yours?

_____

_____

_____

_____

Are there other adopted children in your family?

_____

_____

_____

_____

The parents went off to have tea and coffee and discuss adoption, while the children shyly settled into their chairs. Mrs. Bright spoke first.

"Welcome to the first meeting of The Adoption Club. I realized so many children at our school were adopted so I thought you would like to gather and talk."

Mr. Jackman, everyone's favorite history teacher, smiled.

"I volunteered to help because I was adopted when I was a baby. When I was adopted, my birth parents and adoptive parents never met. It was called a closed adoption. I was 34 before I met my birth parents."

The children looked at their feet. They never heard an adult who was adopted talk about it before. A million questions were in their minds about birth parents and how everyone came into their family.

Do you know any adopted adults?

_____

_____

_____

_____

Have you ever asked them about their adoption?

_____

_____

_____

_____

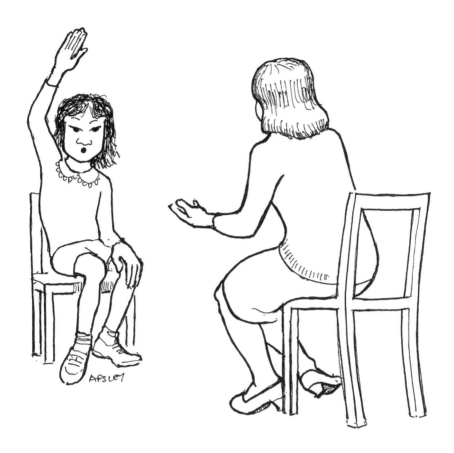

Mrs. Bright smiled again.

"Before we talk about serious topics like birth parents, do any of you want to share your adoption story?"

Mary raised her hand.

"I was adopted from China by my mom. Everyone knows I am adopted because my mom is White and I am Asian. Sometimes kids tease me about being adopted and being a different race. I was three years old when I came to my mom. She is single so I have no dad in this family and I am the only child. I am ten right now. I was left by my birth family by the post office in China and then I went to an orphanage."

Do you look like your adopted family?

_____

When did you come to your adoptive family? How old were you?

_____

_____

Do people know when they see you that you are adopted?

_____

_____

_____

_____

Has anyone teased you about being adopted?

_____

_____

_____

_____

Alexander wiggled in his chair. He was surprised that Mary was also in an orphanage. He began to speak.

"I was adopted from Russia so I was in an orphanage too. I was adopted by my dad when I was five years old. Sometimes kids tease me about having only a dad but no one knows I am adopted unless I tell them. I kind of look like my adoptive dad.

"I didn't like the orphanage. Sometimes there was not enough food. I was afraid no one wanted me and I would be there forever. I am eleven now so finally I have been with my dad longer than I was in Russia. I was scared when I came to my family because I couldn't speak English."

ER/2278110

Do you remember coming to your family?

_____

_____

Were you sad? Scared? Glad? Angry?

_____

_____

_____

_____

_____

If you were too young to remember, how do you think you felt?

_____

_____

_____

_____

Alice said, "My adoption is a lot different. My mom and dad had a son already who was born to them. They picked me up at the hospital when I was a few days old. My birth mother and father are Mexican and Puerto Rican and they picked my adoptive family. I visit my birth parents a few times a year. I am nine and sometimes I wonder if my parents love my brother more since he was their birth child. I think they are fair but I do wonder."

Do you have brothers or sisters through adoption?

_____

_____

Do you feel like your parents treat everyone fairly?

_____

_____

_____

_____

*Do you ever wonder if your birth parents had other children
and that you might have birth siblings you never met?*

_____

_____

_____

_____

_____

Michael looked down at his feet. He didn't want to share his story but his sister Angela raised her hand.

"Michael and I were adopted together from foster care. Our birth parents loved us but had problems and didn't always take care of us. We were in several foster homes, and once we were separated. I hated that. We were adopted by one family. We were older when adopted. I was eight and Michael was twelve. We have been in our family one year."

Were you in any foster homes?

_____

_____

What were they like?

_____

_____

_____

Were you adopted by your foster parents?

_____

_____

_____

Were you ever separated from your sibling?

_____

_____

_____

_____

The last child in the group was Robert. He started talking.

"I am twelve also. My birth parents couldn't take care of me because of my disability. My aunt and uncle adopted me. It is called a kinship adoption because someone related to me adopted me. I don't see my birth mother anymore but I still see my birth father. My aunt is his sister. I came to my family when I was two. I call my aunt and uncle 'Mom' and 'Dad.' They have four birth children so we are a big family. They are talking about adopting another child."

Do you visit any of your birth family?

_____

_____

_____

_____

Is your family large like Robert's?

_____

_____

_____

_____

Draw a picture of your family below.

Mrs. Bright looked at the clock.

"I think we need a break. It is time for a snack."

As the children went to the snack table, Michael scowled at Angela. He did not like sharing his story, and he thought she had a big mouth. He was not happy to be in the group.

Has anyone ever asked you questions about adoption that you didn't want to answer?

_____

_____

_____

_____

Do you share your story?

_____

_____

_____

_____

Who do you share it with?

_____

_____

_____

_____

APSLEY

After cookies and juice, the children gathered again. Mr. Jackman began to talk.

"I can't believe that there are so many different ways to be adopted. When I was a child I thought I was the only adopted child in the universe. Thank you for sharing. I see some people are having big feelings and questions about adoption."

Which character in The Adoption Club has an adoption like yours?

_____

_____

_____

Does your adoptive family match any of their families? Describe how they are similar.

_____

_____

_____

_____

_____

_____

_____

_____

_____

Mr. Jackman said, "One thing I know you all have in common is that you all have a birth mother and a birth father. I wonder if you ever think of them."

Mary spoke first. "I wonder all the time what they look like."

Alexander chimed in, "And I wonder why they didn't keep me."

Alice said, "I didn't know other children didn't visit their birth parents. I can ask mine anything."

Robert said, "I am glad I see my birth dad and I do have pictures of my birth mom so I know what she looks like. I do worry about her and wonder where she is. I hope she is all right."

Angela said, "We lived with our birth parents a long time so we know a lot about them. I wish they could have done what they needed to do to keep us."

Michael didn't say anything.

What do you know about your birth parents?

_____

_____

_____

_____

_____

_____

_____

_____

_____

_____

Can you draw a picture of them? If you don't know what they look like, draw a picture of what you imagine.

What else would you like to know?

_____

_____

_____

_____

_____

Who could help you find out more?

_____

_____

_____

How often do you think about your birth parents?

_____

_____

_____

_____

_____

APSCEY

Michael suddenly stood up. He shouted, "I don't like my sister talking about our birth parents. It makes me very angry. I still love them a lot and don't want people to talk about them." He shoved his chair away from his sister and then sat down again.

Robert looked up. "I am angry sometimes about my birth parents. They could have learned about my disability like my aunt and uncle did."

Mary said, "I am mostly sad. China has all kinds of policies about babies and I don't understand them."

Alexander said, "Sometimes I am scared. When I grow up I want to find them and I am scared they will be dead before I can or that I will never find them."

Alice said, "I am glad I can still see them and that they picked a good family for me."

When you think about your birth parents do you have one feeling or lots of different feelings?

_____

_____

Are you glad, sad, angry or scared?

_____

_____

_____

Draw a picture to show how you sometimes feel.

If you do not see your birth parents, do you want to find them one day? What would you say? Write your answer in the speech bubble below.

APSLEY

Mr. Jackman said, "All those feelings are all right. You may have different feelings at different times. The important thing is to share these feelings with your parents."

Angela said, "I am scared to share sometimes. I love my adoptive parents, but I love my birth parents too. I don't want to hurt my adoptive parents' feelings by talking about my birth parents."

Mr. Jackman smiled. "I felt like that when I was a child. I kept all my feelings inside and then sometimes I couldn't control them anymore and I would burst like a volcano. I learned to share feelings with my parents. It helps make my problems smaller."

Michael looked at Mr. Jackman. "I am sorry I shouted," he said.

Mr. Jackman said, "It is OK to have feelings. Thank you for apologizing. Talking about birth parents can be hard."

Do you talk to your adoptive parents about your birth parents?

_____

_____

_____

_____

_____

_____

Mr. Jackman and Mrs. Bright began to set out some boxes, markers, glitter, stickers and other craft supplies.

Mr. Jackman said, "Some children, like Robert and Alice, see their birth parent or parents. Others do not. Some children like to make a box for their birth mother, birth father or both. They decorate it and then put in school pictures, a postcard from a trip, holiday cards, notes, questions or other items they want to share. Then, if they do search for their birth parents they have a gift to give. Anyone want to work on this?"

All the children agreed they would like to do this. They didn't know what the future would bring but this gave them a place to put some of their feelings.

The parents filed in to help with the boxes and all agreed that The Adoption Club was a place they enjoyed.

Do you want to make a birth parent box?

What would you like to put into it? Draw some pictures.

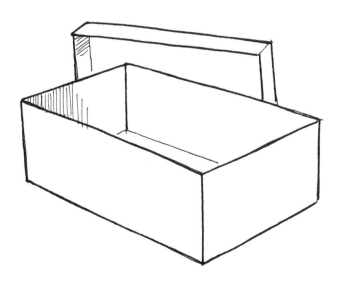

RESOURCES

Your child might enjoy

Brodzinsky, Anne Braff (2013) *Can I tell you about Adoption?* London, UK: Jessica Kingsley Publishers.

Grossnickle, Mary (2014) *A Place in My Heart.* London, UK: Jessica Kingsley Publishers.

Kupecky, Regina and Mitchell, Christine (2000) *A Foster-Adoption Story: Angela and Michael's Journey.* San Francisco, CA: Publisher: Authors.

Peacock, Carol Antoinette and Costello Brownell, Shawn (2000) *Mommy Far, Mommy Near: An Adoption Story.* Parkridge, IL: Albert Whitman & Co.

Oelschlager, Vanita (2010) *Porcupette Finds a Family.* Akron, OH: Vanita Books.

Adults might enjoy

Kupecky, Regina and Keck, Gregory (1995) *Adopting the Hurt Child.* Colorado Springs, CO: Piñon Press.

Kupecky, Regina and Keck, Gregory (2002) *Parenting the Hurt Child.* Colorado Springs, CO: NavPress.

Verrier, Nancy Newton (1993) *The Primal Wound: Understanding the Adopted Child.* Baltimore, VA: Gateway Press.

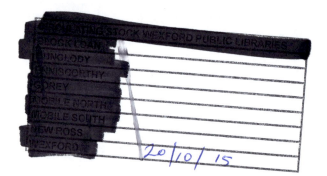